Baby Forest Animals

Jane Katirgis

Bailey Books
an imprint of
Enslow Publishers, Inc.
40 Industrial Road
Box 398
Berkeley Heights, NJ 07922
USA
http://www.enslow.com

Bailey Books, an imprint of Enslow Publishers, Inc.

Copyright © 2011 by Enslow Publishers, Inc.

Library of Congress Cataloging-in-Publication Data

Katirgis, Jane.
 Baby forest animals / Jane Katirgis.
   p. cm. — (All about baby animals)
 ISBN 978-0-7660-3798-4
 1. Forest animals—Infancy—Juvenile literature. 2. Forest animals—Pictorial works
—Juvenile literature. I. Title.
 QL112.K36 2011
 591.73—dc22   2010019741
 Paperback ISBN: 978-1-59845-161-0

Printed in the United States of America

052010 Lake Book Manufacturing, Inc., Melrose Park, IL

10 9 8 7 6 5 4 3 2 1

To Our Readers: We have done our best to make sure all Internet Addresses in this book
were active and appropriate when we went to press. However, the author and the publisher
have no control over and assume no liability for the material available on those Internet sites
or on other Web sites they may link to. Any comments or suggestions can be sent by e-mail
to comments@enslow.com or to the address on the back cover.

♻ Enslow Publishers, Inc., is committed to printing our books on recycled paper. The paper
in every book contains 10% to 30% post-consumer waste (PCW). The cover board on the
outside of each book contains 100% PCW. Our goal is to do our part to help young people
and the environment too!

Photo Credits: iStockphoto.com: © Dirk Freder, pp. 3 (family), 22, © George Clerk, p. 20,
© Mark Kostich, pp. 1, 8, 10, © S. Greg Panosian, p. 12; Pete Oxford/ Minden Pictures, p. 16;
Shutterstock.com, pp. 3 (baby, forest), 4, 6, 14, 18.

Cover Photo: © Mark Kostich / iStockphoto.com

Note to Parents and Teachers
Help pre-readers get a jumpstart on reading. These lively stories introduce simple concepts
with repetition of words and short simple sentences. Photos and illustrations fill the pages
with color and effectively enhance the text. Free Educator Guides are available for this series
at www.enslow.com. Search for the *All About Baby Animals* series name.

Contents

Words to Know

baby   family   forest

In the forest, what do you see?

I see a baby.

I see a baby.

I see a baby.

I see a baby.

I see a baby.

I see a baby.

I see a baby.

In the forest, what do you see?

21

I see a family.

Read More

Aloian, Molly, and Bobby Kalman. *A Rainforest Habitat.*
   New York : Crabtree Pub. Co., 2007.

Willis, Jeanne. *Gorilla! Gorilla!* New York: Atheneum, 2006.

Web Sites

Enchanted Learning. *All About Rainforests.*
<http://www.enchantedlearning.com/subjects/rainforest>

National Wildlife Federation. *Wildlife Watch.*
<http://www.nwf.org/wildlifewatch/>

Index

Guided Reading Level: B
Guided Reading Leveling System is based on the guidelines
recommended by Fountas and Pinnell.

Word Count: 46